SAND MAGIC
EXPERIENCE IN MINIATURE:
A NON-VERBAL THERAPY FOR CHILDREN

S0-AFH-717

JEANNETTE PRUYN REED, M.A.
PSYCHOLOGIST

Jeanette P. Reed
37365 2nd St NeahKahnie
Nehalem, OR 97131

PRIVATELY PRINTED
JPR, PUBLISHERS
722 Silver Avenue S.E.
Albuquerque, New Mexico 87102

FIRST PRINTNG

© JEANNETTE PRUYN REED 1975

LIBRARY OF CONGRESS CARD NO. 75-15117

ALL RIGHTS RESERVED

NO QUOTATION OR TRANSLATIONS
OR OTHER PARTS OF THIS BOOK
MAY BE USED WITHOUT EXPRESS
CONSENT OF THE AUTHOR

6.39

TO CHARLOTTE KLAHN
WITH THANKS

ACKNOWLEDGMENTS

My introduction to the Sandbox Magic Technique was through a colleague and friend—Evelyn Dundas. She told me of Dr. Harold Stone's work with children. I visited his office in Los Angeles and became convinced of its therapeutic value. Dora Kalff came to Los Angeles from Zurich for a seminar at that time, which I attended. Later I studied with her in Zurich.

Sand Magic is the result of many years of observation of The Exceptional Child—bright, average, retarded; physically, neurologically or emotionally disturbed. The children mentioned are grown now and identification is no longer possible or threatening.

I am grateful to many people who worked with me during the time we were pioneering at the Special Education Center and Day School for Exceptional Children.

Especially to my father, Francis Lansing Pruyn, who made it financially possible. To Kathrine Simons who encouraged my writing. To Dr. Stuart Adler, pediatrician, who accepted the responsibility of Medical Director in 1950 and supervised the program and directed our work. To Dr. Lucie Gale McMurray, pediatrician and specialist in the field of Exceptional Children, who supervised and encouraged our work at the Center since 1963. Her understanding of our methods and program gave me courage to persevere. To Dr. Ross Snyder, Child Psychiatrist, who donated his time in many cases and fortified our program. To Charlotte Klahn, who as a student and trainee, helped formulate many of the ideas. She edited and typed the manuscript.

TABLE OF CONTENTS

A GENERAL SURVEY
of
PLAY THERAPY

The following pages outline the principles of play therapy as a technique used in child guidance and psychotherapy. Virginia Axline and her teacher Carl Rogers were the progenitors of this therapeutic field.

Explanation of Process Psychotherapy in child guidance is a fusion of psychoanalytically oriented psychiatry and social therapies. The treatment plan or design derives from a flexible evaluation of the functioning of the total personality. Psychotherapy in family and child guidance always concerns itself with the family constellation, not merely as environment for the "patient." For the child, the line is less easy to draw, more of the unconscious usually being brought into the therapeutic process and ego building. Indirect therapy is used in various combinations: (a) expressing unconscious drives; (b) minimizing the effect of the repressive super-ego or building a super-ego (depending upon whether the problem is more one of anxiety or acting out); (c) adapting to concepts of reality, both as represented by the person or therapist and the outer world. Whenever drives are released, the child must also be helped to measure himself in the real world or confusion will result.

The essence of child guidance lies in the combination of varying proportions of direct psychotherapy and social therapies. The child brings his reality into the interview, but the therapist also reaches out into the child's world through contact with those most concerned with his problem. When parental attitudes cannot be modified, removing the child from the conditions of pressure may result in improvement if a favorable therapeutic attitude in substitute parental figures can be induced. A child with a sense of failure in school can be helped if his program can be modified and his teachers' attitudes made more tolerant. Necessary in both above cases is the direct therapeutic effort, geared for self-awareness and self-direction.

The Therapeutic Attitude The central dynamic in all psychotherapy may be regarded as permissiveness—a special kind of love called acceptance. Ordinarily, parents give their children more acceptance than will be given them in the outside world. The therapist is not a parent or a substitute parent, yet he may play a "parental" role. He must be a good friend, but not a friend in the ordinary social sense. The therapist is never the real love object, though the patient, especially the child, so regards him during the period of treatment.

The "role" of the therapist consists of warmth, concern, therapeutic understanding and interest in helping the person to get well. This is a clinical or professional development of a natural quality. The therapist does not give love in the ordinary sense. He must show approval or disapproval when the occasion arises. His diagnostic sense guides him in expressing and timing his effort to gratify and to support the patient. Consistency, neutrality, firmness as well as warmth enter into the therapeutic relationship.

Transference In child guidance, the problem is by hypothesis already emotionally charged so that a transference relationship of some intensity is essential. In the therapeutic process, the therapist by accepting behavior with a tolerant, friendly and permissive attitude, induces a basic, positive transference within which currents of negative, positive and mixed feelings may run. This basic, positive transference holds throughout the period of treatment.

In psychotherapy, the identity of the therapist is purposefully kept vague so that the patient can use the therapist fully according to his own inner needs, thus permitting a wide range of displacements. The relationship permits the client to reveal himself, discharge his tensions, unleash his emotions and bring fear and aggression to the surface. Through this experience, he may be helped to better understand himself and his world of reality. In addition, transference is used for emotional support when the ego is weak, when the defensive structure should be maintained or when there are rigid personality structures. Deeply fixed childish traits, severe illness (mental or physical) or deficient intelligence may also require a firm supportive transference.

Dynamics of Change To understand the process of therapy, one must recall what happened to the child in past familiar surroundings. In the little child, satisfactions are magically brought about by the parents. In the gradual socialization of the child, as he grows out of his narcissisms, the parents who are too powerful for him to oppose, become the perfect figures. By trying to imitate them, the child overcomes his insecurity. This identification of the same sex, is particularly achieved during the oedipal phases. It is repeated and finally stabilized during adolescence. In normal development, during which identification becomes possible because of the parents' sustaining love and wise prohibition, the child is integrated and able to establish object relationships with others. In less normal development, capacity to relate is dependent, ambivalent, or at its poorest level, narcissistic or infantile.

In therapy, the stages of constructive identification have still to be reached by the client and are now achieved in the experience itself. The transference permits the child "to regress" to the earlier levels of development. With the therapist, the child is able to make a fresh start on the problem of constructive identification. He reproduces or repeats his emotional reactions of an earlier age. All the conflicts he has had in the past—either negative or positive—which have gone beyond their limits of time are allowed to be resolved. Those patterns are affected by the permissive, tolerant attitude of the therapist, and the child is forced into a new attitude which is free from distortions. He can draw on his own potential strength for insight and change.

Resistance Resistance shows itself as an interruption of the client's expressing himself. This automatically develops as soon as the transference is established. When the defenses are removed and the therapist approaches the center of emotional conflict, the client fears that the therapist will now frustrate and reject him. The child may discontinue his modelling or destroy it or burst into silly talk. There is a definite disturbance of the flow between the therapist and child. One has to make clear to him that he is repeating an old pattern. Only if this pattern can be interrupted can energies be set free.

Release Techniques Living out feelings in motor activities and verbal or non-verbal expression is natural for young children, and discussion of feelings in play or in the interview tends toward gradual desensitization. Desensitization takes place slowly when the client becomes free enough and strong enough in the transference to bring disturbing feelings out. He may then feel free to express anxiety about experiences in actual life.

11

In phases of simple release during non-verbal play, the role of the therapist may be quite minimal (or even passive). In most guidance cases where the disturbance is pervasive and showing itself through many symptoms, simple release is not enough. In play, the impulse is actually discharged, so that the conflict is realistically "lived out." The reduction of the intensity of conflict makes it possible to move on instead of being entrenched in old patterns. For young children or inhibited children, who have not attained the usual levels of body mastery and skill, motor release in itself is of therapeutic importance. (I have noticed this fact through my work with the "problem" child in a regular school environment and have aimed much of the work in this direction through "Sing It and Do It"[1] activities.)

The Supportive Relationship Insight is not always achieved and cannot always be the aim. Support is used as a phase of treatment with many disturbed children. It has the purpose of reinforcement through warmth and friendliness. By these attitudes one may encourage self dependence and efforts at reality adjustment, but change in personality may not occur. Authoritative firmness is sometimes used by the therapist when the parent needs reinforcement in carrying through a wise decision for his child or himself.

For little children, release of feelings in a supportive relationship may be self-healing if the parental attitudes can be modified and environmental conditions made more favorable for growth.

The Meaning and Use of Play The distinguishing technique in therapy for young children is in the use of imagination in play. Play is used because the young child is best able to express himself through activity. Play offers opportunity for growth, for release of tension, for practice in new achievements, for reality testing and for development. Through it, the child learns how to meet new situations, to increase his motility, to bring together fantasy and reality —distinguishing the two, to build ego strength and to dilute frightening and traumatic events by reproducing them in harmless disguises.

Play is used to reach the child on whatever level he finds himself. Play is also used both because it is the little child's medium of communication and because it provides in a safe and natural way

---

[1] *See Jeannette P. Reed, "Sing It and Do It," biblio.*

some of the instinctual gratification needed by the child as he learns to meet reality demands.

Play Materials and Setting The play materials used in a guidance agency are those long tested in ordinary living as appropriate for the particular age range. The universality of the appeal rests on the universality of the motivation. The basic toys which reflect levels of development become channels for expressing the whole personality. Sandbox, clay, plasticene, shells, buttons and water all offer to the young child easy access to his unsolved problems. He can enjoy his messiness and satisfy his original impulses in acceptable forms. There are also available, cannons, soldiers, guns, darts and knives for the display of aggression; blocks and other materials for constructing and building; water and paint as outlets for toilet problems and for creative activities; the doll family for study of relationships; clay and paint crayons to express the ideation; and so forth. Older children not only use paints, but leather and tools for self-expression and "acting out." In general, the child is allowed to play, as long as he will with one set of toys rather than be exposed to a great many, so that he may develop his own ideas and fantasies.

The sandbox is a legitimate branch of play therapy. Its use is more widely understood in Europe, and until recent years, it was not utilized in the United States. This book is primarily directed towards introducing and expanding the use of the Sandbox Miniature Technique as implemented and observed through case studies of exceptional children at the Special Education Center and Albuquerque Hearing and Speech Center in Albuquerque, New Mexico.

INTRODUCTION

To form, create, express, pioneer and experience are universal urges. Energy must be used and renewed by one method or another. It must be directed and redirected. It constellates, resolves, evolves and reforms endlessly. Psychic energy follows the same paths as physical energy. This becomes evident in varying ways. The exceptional child as well as one who is "normal" will benefit greatly by using his hands. Manipulating clay, blocks, water/finger paint and sand are important tools. The direct contact with the elements and the tactile processes alone—earth (sand), water and even fire in controlled experimentation—will have a therapeutic effect.

The above mentioned methods have been used in Play Therapy for many years. Lauretta Bender* and Virginia Axline* are noted therapists who have advocated Art and Permissive (non-directive) therapy and have proved their value through extensive practice. I have used these media in conjunction with exceptional children of all types and find them formative as well as developmental tools.

I would like to add the Sandbox Miniature Technique to the above approaches. It is an outgrowth of "The World Test," originated by Margaret Lowenfeld* in England; and developed by Dora Kalff,* in Zurich, Charlotte Buhler,* in New York and Dr. Harold Stone,* in Los Angeles. Edith Sullwold of Los Angeles is a gifted therapist who has also been influenced by these people.

Refer to Bibliography.

HISTORY

The Sandbox Miniature Technique was first used in 1928 by Dr. Margaret Lowenfeld at the Institute of Child Psychology in England. She and other members of her staff were interested in, and developed a technique for studying non-verbal communication of children. She called this study "World Pictures of Children." Her equipment included miniatures of living creatures, fantasy figures, scenery, transport machinery and equipment and other objects. She explained that this was a natural way of "thinking" and that it would help bridge the two worlds of childhood and adulthood. The child was told to do whatever came into his head. She felt the World Technique was an agent of communication. It was characterized as being multi-dimensional, having dynamic possibilities and having the power to present states of mind not before known. Additionally, the technique would not require any special skills in execution.

In 1935, Dr. Charlotte Buhler saw the World Technique and then in 1949 developed it and brought it to the United States as "The World Test" which she used diagnostically. Dora Kalff of Zurich has used this technique for the same purpose as well as therapeutically. Her book, *Sandplay*, describes her work. She has trained many people the world over, including Japan, Switzerland and America. Another therapist, Edith Sullwold, has worked with both Dr. Stone and Dora Kalff developing her own techniques.

My training with Dora Kalff, in Zurich, helped me to realize the possibilities of the sandbox with exceptional and handicapped children.

PHYSICAL SET-UP

The Sandbox Technique is *experience* in miniature. It is dynamic, dramatic and, to the child, very real. The sandbox itself is a controlled space in which there are opportunities to build, shape, change, imagine, order, simplify, perfect and embellish a concept or an idea in wet or dry sand. Two wooden boxes are made available, 23" by 28" and 4" deep, in a cheerful, small comfortable room. The height of the boxes from the floor may vary according to the age of the child. Rollers on the feet of the table make the box more accessible. A TV stand is a practical vehicle for the sandbox. The medium is sand. It is fluid, pliable and formable with endless manipulative opportunities. Two boxes are painted blue to simulate water when all the sand is pushed away. They should be lined with heavy, clear plastic so that real water may be used and safely contained. One box is dry sand and one is damp sand. The child's choice of media is a vital part of therapy.

Miniatures of all kinds; prehistoric, wild and domestic animals, shells, stones and trees, birds and insects, vehicles for transportation, army soldiers, tents, cannons, tanks, ships, bridges, caves, houses or other small community figures, people and religious and fantasy reproductions are placed on shelves near at hand, ready to be *chosen.*

DIRECTIONS FOR PROCEDURE

The child expresses a desire to work in the sand. In a school situation, he may be taken from regular activities as a special privilege, or abstracted from the classroom if he is causing a disturbance. The child, upon entering, looks around and usually has an idea. He may handle the sand before choosing between wet or dry. By finding the objects to complement and effect that idea the child finds immediate satisfaction. The project grows. It may be embellished and added to. Additional concepts usually succeed each other. An accompanying story enhances the child's creation.

Verbalization is important, though not essential. Consciously or unconsciously, a form evolves and one recognizes the child's relative ability. I have noticed that the brighter child will produce a sandbox "picture" using more imagination and ingenuity than the less gifted child or child with a handicap. Meagre ideation and lack of ingenuity are adversely proportional to concrete expression. In reference to meagre ideation, the child usually has less colorful, fewer and underdeveloped concepts. The form is less firm. The objects chosen are simple, concrete and banal. Verbalization is apt to be sparse or in a monotone, the story less rich and clear. Progress is slower and regression is more frequent. Perseveration may continue for a longer period of time (plateau) or recur more frequently Finally, if and when a change does occur, it is less evident. It has become clear to me through the sandbox that the brain damaged child fits into the last description, whereas the emotionally disturbed child may show more rapid and consistent progress. Through verbal

17

or non-verbal communication one gains insight into the child's difficulties. Returning to previous school activities, the child is relaxed, exhibits more appropriate behavior and is prepared to concentrate on academics. The same will apply to a child in a clinical situation, measured by his behavior at home and at school.

INTERPRETATION AND PROCESS

The advantages of sandbox techniques are as follows:

1. It permits the child to form his own concept which he is then able to express concretely.
2. He enjoys making the sandbox "picture" and usually enjoys explaining it.
3. He learns to accept the limitations of time, space and materials.
4. He can see and feel the completed picture, immediately or in the future.
5. He can show and relate his ideas to the therapist, teacher and friends.

The unusual or gifted child will profit through creative experiences. Progress will be evident as expression takes place—verbally or non-verbally. Improvement in behavior may also manifest itself in other media, but the sandbox miniatures are a stimulus to the child's imagination, which is evidenced through his use and choice of objects. Alterations in sand form may denote or predict an unconscious movement towards growth as one is on the lookout, for the relative behavior will have a message. One will be able to understand symbolically what is occurring in relation to school social behavior, academic progress and behavior at home. This substantiates the idea that children have within themselves the power and ability to bring about their own therapy. The innate healing process is quite often suppressed or overlooked. In summation, improved form, color and logic; growth in imagination and ingenuity; enriched choice and arrangement of objects, as well as more complex verbal description, indicate progress.

"One thing must be kept in mind, the sandbox is no substitute for the human encounter! The child is given the opportunity to express himself

*non-verbally. Someone must be on hand to re-
ceive his production. As I have worked with
these children and gradually introduced the sandbox, I find they are more and more able to express their deep fantasy life to bring to the
conscious level some of their hidden fears, anger
or aggressive feelings. Creativity unfolds and a
general growth process occurs. Daydreams can
be expressed in concrete form, ridding the child
of what he or she feels is threatening. If the child
has an emotional block to learning, his attitude
may be changed and improved through the experience in miniature. In using the sandbox technique we are studying some of the manifestations
of the child's feelings and psyche."* [2]

It must be thoroughly understood and accepted that if one is
going to study children and work with them, the therapist must
first learn about himself, in order that he or she will not make the
mistake of correcting faults in children that may well be reflection
or projection of themselves. It is important for the therapist to
realize that with each additional sandbox sequence he will develop
insight, gain experience and, inevitably, his own technique will
emerge. More meaningful and richer interpretation will result.

*"As Jung pointed out in his essay on the
development of the personality, there are too
many people who want to study children without
first learning about themselves. Naturally, we
never know ourselves fully, and this certainly
cannot be a requirement for beginning a serious
study of the child. What I think is necessary on
the part of the adult, especially the adult who
deals with children intimately (which includes
just about everyone), is an introspective attitude
towards one's own psychology. One has to be
open to an investigation of one's own psychol-*

[2] *The ideas expressed, here, were introduced to me by personal communication with Evelyn Dundas, a therapist who uses the Sandbox Technique in
Oakland, California, and in presentations by Edith Sullwold.*

ogy. One has to be open to an investigation of one's own problems and complexes, for otherwise the full weight of our critical faculties is brought to bear on the child, and we expect too much of him." [3]

RECORDING

Photographing of each sand "picture" is important. The sequence of slides or pictures indicates quite clearly where the individual "is" in his process of growth, adjustment or readjustment. The same child may also benefit by seeing his pictures in the future. He can see that his efforts are not lost. His creations have been received and valued. Diagrams, if preferred, may be used in addition to or in place of photos.

Notes taken are as important as the photos, slides or diagrams. The child's story as well as the therapist's observations, add to the complete record. The initial sandbox is often valuable as a diagnostic tool. The sequence will be useful as an indication of growth, *change* or development. It may reflect the feelings, non-verbally, that the child has not been able to express. The sandbox provides us with a key to interpret his non-adaptive behavior at home, in the classroom, or in various less structured surroundings. It is of value to teacher, therapist and counselor to note changes and developments of characteristic behavior patterns indicated by the sequence of sandbox records.

---

[3] *Harold Stone, "The Child: His Mind and His Imagination."*

THE SANDBOX MINIATURE TECHNIQUE

AS A DIAGNOSTIC TOOL FOR EXCEPTIONAL CHILDREN

In using varying techniques of psycho-therapy with exceptional children at the Special Education Center,* I have accidentally touched upon a valuable approach for verifying and confirming the diagnostic evaluations of children with complex problems presently called "Learning Disabilities." "Minimal brain dysfunction," "emotional disturbance," "hyperactivity" and "retarded" are terms used to describe these young ones. Diffused damage or minimal brain dysfunction are difficult to identify. It is important to detect, identify and pinpoint their difficulties at an early age, in order to outline their therapy and educational program. The E.E.G. and other tests; psychological, educational, neurological, the Graham-Kendall for possible brain damage, and the Bender-Gestalt for organic or emotional difficulties, help to confirm findings of the physician, neurologist, psychologist or psychiatrist. Lately, the ITPA (Illinois Test of Psycholinguistic Abilities) is of special value in correlating the perceptual defects with other tests. An additional projective approach which I have been using for diagnosis and therapy is the Sandbox Miniature Technique.

At the Center, we are fortunate to have had children with many types of learning difficulties or other problems sent in for evaluation, observation and therapy. Their one common denominator is that they cannot learn or function in a public or private school situation. The reasons are multiple and varied. It is our purpose to evaluate and study these children, in order to outline individual remedial programs that will benefit each child and return him to the "average" groups and regular schools.

Through several years of work I observed a dichotomy of results in the Sandbox Miniature Technique. Studying the photographs in sequence of the children's sand experiences, I observed that:

The rate of change in behavior:
—varied .... was blocked

The subject matter:
—differed .... remained the same

The arrangement:
—changed .... remained static

The arrangement of objects:
—acquired logic .... remained chaotic
—increased in ingenuity .... remained rudimentary

When the sandbox is used as a diagnostic tool, I have become increasingly aware of different results:

1. A child who is emotionally disturbed with no apparent brain dysfunction noted by an E.E.G., neurological tests and/or no score on the Graham-Kendall Tests for Memory of Design, or the Bender-Gestalt test, will normally create pictures showing progress in arrangement, logical patterns and design.

2. The pictures of a child with physical disability, such as minimal brain dysfunction, central nervous system damage, spinal bifida or post natal accident remain jumbled without sequence and without logic. Perseveration is usual. Change is rare and unusual.

3. If a child has a minimal brain dysfunction as well as noticeable emotional disturbance, the pictures may evolve and progress, *if* and *when* the neurological difficulty begins to resolve. The emotional problem will also improve if this occurs. The following scale may be useful as a diagnostic tool —graphs may eventually be made of each scale to measure and evaluate each child's picture in these terms. (Refer to pages 28 and 29 for the scale.)

4. The emotionally disturbed child (schizophrenic or autistic) will show quite a different sequential picture. Fantasy will be more prominent. In the autistic child, language is apt to improve and become logical.

Occasionally, the change was startling or spontaneous after months of perseveration. For the emotionally disturbed child this was usually indicative of change, observed in his behavior at home or by improved learning ability at school. The brain damaged child showed perseveration and rarely changed arrangement of materials even through a lapse of weeks of intermittent therapy. Logic seemed to be absent, confusion of arrangement was evident and there was little change in choice of materials. Any indication of change became evident slowly through motor co-ordination or improved behavior.

Methods of therapy, whatever forms they may take, have for their goal the improvement in functioning, or correction of faulty patterns of growth and behavior of the individual.

Play therapy, as introduced by Virginia Axline in her book, *Play Therapy*, is a method widely employed by psycho-therapists for children who are experientially deprived or in need of emotional outlets or controls. Verbalization is encouraged. Free choice of materials and laissez faire approach is usual, combined with guidance and observation for the purpose of evaluation of progress.

Changes in behavior can be accomplished through varied creative approaches and techniques (i.e. dance, art, music, puppets and drama) as outlined in *Child Psychiatric Techniques*, by Lauretta Bender[4] and others who stress creative activities in both learning and relearning.

I was exposed to the Sandbox Miniature Technique (a projective approach and derivative of the Lowenfeld World Test) as developed by Dr. Harold Stone, psychologist in private practice in Los Angeles, and Professor at the University of California, and studied with Mrs. Dora Kalff of Zurich, Switzerland.

The idea that art methods were being used therapeutically intrigued me sufficiently to ask Dr. Stone for an interview. After seeing Dr. Stone's work, I was convinced of the value of his approach to child therapy and of the importance of the Sandbox Miniature Technique. I felt that the three-dimensional approach within a controlled space was more effective and meaningful to a child than verbalization and free play.

Energy can and must be expressed, controlled and channeled. It is so frequently disorganized in the emotionally disturbed child. To give him an opportunity to express this energy and utilize it constructively is even more important than for the average creative child. Also, the disturbed child is often hampered by his inability to verbalize his feelings directly or adequately. The symbolic non-verbal language of the Sandbox Miniature Technique serves as an important factor in such cases.

Miniatures of all kinds, found on easily accessible shelves, are used by the child to express concepts concerning inner feelings. The child's individual problems will become obvious through perseveration or unusual emphasis indicating conflicts, blocking, or nonverbalized complexes.

After the picture is finished to the child's satisfaction, a photograph is made and numbered. Much can be interpreted from observing the photographs or slides in sequence and studying the choice of materials used, the arrangements and the possible changes or reversals of attitudes which are made evident and *tell* the story as it emerges.

Archaeology, anthropology and sociology are three avenues which plot the development of man in retrospect. The sandbox can do this symbolically, whether or not the symbols or myths are recognized by the therapist. The sandbox is of value to the individual using it. The process of development or therapy goes on regardless of the recognition and analysis. In broad terms, whether or not we understand what is happening to the child is not as important as the realization that the child is making, creating or completing a concept of his own. The importance lies in the *process* and in its effect on the individual, regardless of age, problem, or degree of intelligence, education and experience. The fact that a constructive problem presents itself in a controlled area intrigues the child (or adult) and motivates his creative faculties to a point of activity, initiating effort, organizing energy and forming a concept at whatever level that individual may be. The degree of satisfaction he derives from the encounter will vary and in recurring periods, he will attempt to continue this process, consciously or unconsciously. The unconscious emotional growth, or "integration" process will be understood only by a trained specialist. The conscious expression can be interpreted by an educator, art student or counselor. The child psychologist familiar with either Jungian, Rogerian, or other schools of psychology will be more able to understand the unconscious meanings presented by the "picture in the sand."

It is important to note the intensity and involvement that a child brings to the sandbox experience as it varies from session to session. After a short period of contemplation, he usually immerses himself

24

in his project and identifies strongly with his task. The idea takes form dynamically; his whole body can be observed in action. The tempo indicates the measure of interest involved. At times, quick sharp gestures accomplish his purpose (volcanoes, mounds). Sometimes, strong careful movements carve the idea from the damp sand (ditches, roads or tunnels), or soft flowing movements and delicate strokes form and control the dry mounds (circles, ponds, serpentine or flower-like designs). The dry box is frequently used for designs much as the Indians draw their sand paintings. The medium calls forth skill; with practice the skill improves and satisfaction increases. The experience is definitely therapeutic.

The climate of the situation is important. It is a challenge to the child's ingenuity. It is spontaneous; it is often dynamic or cathartic. It can be simplified or increased in complexity. It is not a static toy whose activity has to be imagined or amplified. It appeals to the kinesthetic sense as well as to the visual and creative senses. It is the individual's own creation; therefore, it is a personal expression of the child's feelings at that particular moment. It can be preserved by photography (slides) and studied again. The photographs can be used as ego reinforcement. Showing and seeing them later increases their value to the child. Giving him a copy of his own creation seems to deepen his satisfaction.

The process will provide the necessary therapy for that individual at his particular level of development. In certain cases of autism, schizophrenia or psychosis, the trained therapist can only interpret what he knows. Practice can increase insight and understanding. The more proficient or knowledgeable he is with the history of man and mythology, the better he will be equipped to capture the meaning of the sand pictures.

We can observe through subsequent behavior of the child whether or not and to what degree change is taking place. "Why," is unimportant as long as it happens.

Gradually, different motifs are introduced, such as trees, plants, vegetation, prehistoric animals, ponds, bridges and families. At this time it becomes apparent that the child's inner needs are being met and can be interpreted through the visual tactile productions he presents. These are non-verbal communications for a complex experience he is as yet unable to verbalize.

The manipulation of the soft dry or wet sand seems to initiate psychic energy and open creative channels. Unconsciously or consciously the story is told in three-dimensional terms. Simultaneously, physical-kinesthetic-visual, and frequently even kinetic forces combine, create and objectify the concept. The direct "feel-think" activity of the child results in release of tension, satisfaction and therapy. The healing process continues and is made evident through behavior at home or carries over to school as improved learning ability. The experience in miniature or concretising of an idea through visual motor activity is a factor in bringing about healing. *+ learning*

In the sandbox, myth, magic and fantasy are set free. They are vital components for enrichment of any imagination and on-going psychological development. This is important to note within the sandbox productions. The child can color his effort with emotional reaction; he can fight, kill, construct or reconstruct, love, hate, enjoy or appreciate. The demythicization of the modern world leaves little to work with in fantasy and imagination. Schools are regimented; sports are organized; work is limited and unionized; rules are made and used as controls for "improved living." Push-button mechanical gadgets are the modern answer to imagining and inventing, but they are dry fodder to the creative child. What will the child's imagination build on psychologically? Past experiences, myth and symbol are his building blocks toward healthy maturity.

The Sandbox Miniature Technique is a valuable tool for this purpose. It can substitute in miniature an experience which has previously been mishandled or has caused a feeling of failure or frustration. It can teach this far better, and possibly less painfully, than the life experience, for it eliminates the problem of an intervening personality—one that has possibly inhibited previous progress through lack of understanding or through too drastic punishment, personal projections or over-expectation. I have known the sandbox to overcome the block caused by an early parent fixation or rejection. It is a constructive media accomplishing many purposes without other guidance than fulfilling the immediate needs of the child. It need not be limited to children; people of all ages profit by working in it, resolving complexes, encouraging growth, ideas and creative approaches to problems through practice and experience. There is much to be said for trial, error and correction which this media permits.

26

Non-verbal communication can be more accurate and informative than verbal. The sandbox encourages and permits verbalization at a deeper level than words. What a child is interested in and how deeply he is concerned about it, his feelings, resentments or his inner wishes become evident in concrete form as he builds in the sandbox. Building a sand picture seems to free him to express in his own language what is uppermost in his mind at the time. We, in turn, can understand him non-verbally through watching him work and by observing the finished product. If he chooses to talk about it, we have the added information we need to interpret his feelings. For this purpose, a tape recording is useful for later study. Expression of the conscious world will be quite evident. The unconscious attitude reveals itself clearly to the trained eye through symbols or signs. No interference should be made during the making of the picture, but rarely does there need to be other than care for the sand or objects "so we can use them again." Since the child may make his own rules, he will understand them and abide by them. Breaking or burning valuable items should not be permitted except for a specific purpose or under extreme conditions.

Several very different approaches can be tried. Either an all- *modes* permissive, protective approach by a warm feminine therapist, or the parallel of the father-pal, male approach—a "go about his own business and work on his own project" attitude is conducive to creative production. The one chosen depends on the child's development level, his age, his problem or need and atttiude towards a parental image. I meet the child on his own level and provide a "feel with" climate. The child is permitted to build his own way and to shape without interference with minimal support. He tells me when he has finished and is ready for a photograph. Each step is vital to the whole and becomes *more* than the whole. It is not *therapy* unless this happens. To direct the process is to deny it meaning and purpose.

Whatever school of psychology one believes in—Jungian, Freudian, Adlerian, Rogerian and their modern derivatives—the interpretation will vary. The essential point is that the child begins to move out of a static emotional state into a new one in which he becomes motivated towards better "integration," "individuation," or "self-actualization." In other words, he redirects his energy, overt or overflowing, to a more controlled and growth-oriented purposive goal. The Sandbox Miniature Technique, as Dora Kalff uses it with her deep knowledge of myth, symbol and anthropology, archaeology, religions, as well as analytical background, is of value in interpreting results.

As one studies the photo slide sequence of a child's sandbox, one notes that aggression and chaos are often the first evidence of inner turmoil or signal for clinical help. The inner frustration, overcontrol, expectation or protection of parents frequently cause these violent expressions of war, killing and wrecking in the sand. Guns, spears, cannons, rockets and atom bombs, in varying degrees of lethal importance, announce the child's rebellion and dissatisfaction with present conditions. He may have been a passive child, a "good child." Nevertheless, in the sandbox, prehistoric and wild animals devour and kill.

When vegetation appears in the picture the child has taken a progressive step towards more suitable behavior although fluctuation and regression may occur. The appearance of water in any form (streams, ponds, rivers, or ocean) indicates the freeing of energy and emotions important to further progress. Dams, tunnels, mounds and caves are indications that energy is collecting. Volcanoes (as in Rorschach) are signs of inner activity! Something is brewing and may explode. Destructive-aggressive feelings are apt to reappear in the form of Indians, cowboys and army paraphernalia. (Opposition or the good-versus-evil theme becomes apparent.)

Man and his products follow in a constructive sense—houses, churches, schools, farms, roads, railroad tracks, aircraft, airports, and boats. Bridges are indications of integration. A weekly or biweekly session with the sandbox will invariably demonstrate that once this is "let out" to the satisfaction of the individual, order, control, pattern and logic begin to show. These changes may or may not be in symbolic terms that *we* understand, but it is evident that a change is occurring. It is important to be aware of the moment when this transition takes place, for the problem may resolve suddenly.

When I studied with Mrs. Kalff in Zurich, I observed an interesting example of this resolution. Slides were shown to us of a case of a boy which had been in process for over seven years, in spite of extreme adverse life situations contributing to severe developmental blocks. His mother died. He lived in foster homes separated from his father, and deep emotional conflict resulted. A group of us were present when the original material was shown. I saw the final picture in the sandbox immediately after its production. Later a slide was shown to the group. From our sessions of viewing the slide series, we had thought a solution impossible because of the circumstances which had been heaped too heavily on this individual. Then, suddenly, he chose his *own* direction. It was the answer to apparently insurmountable problems. There were trees, a garden, flowers, a fountain, a home, a church, a school, people walking around and children playing! This was a remarkable answer to questions that could not have been answered by onyone but the boy himself. He reached a decision, a resolution of problems that had been unsolved for many years, a life direction given in answer to his own quest.

Presently, the young man is doing well and running his father's factory. He is married and living nearby. The case will not end here, but it should develop into a success story in both industry and community living. It renews and strengthens one's faith in the individual to observe such a solution.

To repeat, I find the Sandbox Miniature Technique an invaluable tool with which to measure a child's degree of change, understand his attitudes, problems, interests and observe his attitude towards his immediate needs and problems. Ingenuity, imagination and experiential background are also a measure of his functioning ability or "F.A.Q."

It can be said that any creative or permissive play therapy releases and satisfies the child's emotions, at the time. It is less tangible than the sandbox experience where these feelings may be objectified in concrete form, initiate the rebuilding process. Through the use of the Sandbox Miniature Technique, a child will have the opportunity to begin his ego-journey.

diagnoses

SANDBOX OBSERVATION SCALE FOR CHILDREN

Name of subject:————————————————Date:————————

Therapist:————————————————————B. D.:————————

Number of picture in series:————————————Age:————————

Problem: D.B.D.   E.D.   P.H.   N. Dys.

I. *Approach*   Enthusiastic   Apathetic   Non-Committal
Changes:————————————

II. *Choice of Sand*   Dry   Damp

III. *Orientation*
  A. Handedness: Left   Right   C. Objects closest to where
  B. Worked from: Left to Right   subject stood
                Right to Left   D. Moved around box
                                 E. Worked from same side

IV. *Form*
  a whole logical picture   several ideas
  confused, indifferentiated

V. *Choice of Materials*
  A. People
    1. Human: men, women, children, family
    2. Other than human: fantasy, grotesque, caricatures,
       mythological, symbolic
  B. Animals: prehistoric, wild, domestic, birds, sea creatures,
     amphibious, serpents, dragons—in correct habitat/
     separated
  C. Objects: sea shells, bones, rocks, fossils, jewels,
     vegetation, transportation vehicles, castles, houses,
     churches, war materials, bridges
  D. Geological-Topographical Formation:
    1. Volcanoes, earthquakes
    2. Earth, walls, tunnels, holes, caves
    3. Mountains, hills, lakes, ponds, ocean, water (real)

VI. *Movement—Action*
  People   Animals   Objects   Water (boats, fish)

VII. *Conceptual Level:* Design
  A. Whole Logical Picture
      Sequence   Progress   Perseverate   Regress
      Several Ideas   Confused   Undifferentiated

    B. Change of Idea
       One continuous process (none)   Number of changes———
    C. Overall Theme
       Domestic   Military   Reality   Fantasy   Bizarre
       Destructive   Aggressive

VIII. *Feeling Projected—Impression* (non-verbal-therapist's response to picture)
    A. Colorful   Humorous   Gay   Happy
    B. Confusing   Non-Expressive
    C. Peaceful   Calm
    D. Lacking color   Depressive   Negative
    E. Positive   Spontaneous   Moving

IX. *Creative Level*
    A. All over lay out
       Exceptional   Good   Fair
    B. Ingenuity (adaptation of materials at hand)
       Exceptional   Good   Fair

X. *Verbalization while making the picture*
    Quiet   Some   Constant   Humming
    Story: Taped   Written   Picture

XI. *Subject's response to finished picture*
    Satisfied (Verbally, Visually, Tactilly)   Excited
    Relieved   Proud   Emotional   Indifferent

XII. *Therapist's role*
    Mother   Father
    Casual observed (working independently of subject)
    Assistant (working with subject)
    Co-worker (working on creative expression independent of child)

XIV. *Reason for subject doing a picture*
    Regular time (appointment)   Deviation in behavior
    Suggestion by therapist

NAME:_____AGE:_____

OBSERVER:_____DATE:_____

	POOR	FAIR	GOOD	EXCELLENT
I. ARRANGEMENT LOGIC				
II. CREATIVITY INGENUITY				
III. PERSERVATION				
IV. SYMBOLISM				

OBSERVATIONS: Vegetation   Animals &   Objects; Story
                             Human figures   Geological,
                                              Shells, Rocks,
                                              etc.

INDICATE CHANGE: + = Improvement   — = Regression

INCLUDE IN OBSERVATIONS: Subject's emotion, movements, order of entries, use of whole or part of box
Handedness and direction of work—right, left, circular, etc.

#1

JOHN/*see Page* 41

#2

#3

LARRY/*see Page 45*

#4

#5

MICHAEL/*see Page* 49

#6

#7

WARREN/*see Page 53*

#8

#9

WILLIAM/*see Page 57*

#10

#11

MARIA/*see Page 65*

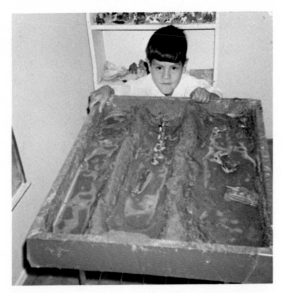

\#12

PEDRO/*see Page 67*

#13

ANDY/*see Page 69*

JOHN
THE MOLE

VISUAL DIFFICULTY

John is eight years old. His intelligence is above average. His ability to abstract and to invent and ingenuity to carry out mechanical projects are unusual. However, HE CANNOT READ! He is slight and thin, with large brown opaque eyes. One cannot read his thoughts: he does not look out. He hides behind them conveniently. His affect is low. He shows no spontaneity usual to a boy of his age. His appetite is poor, and he refuses to eat an average diet. He says he is not hungry. He has been checked by a Pediatrician, a Neurologist (including E.E.G.), and he has had his eyes and ears tested. We have administered the usual psychological and academic tests for evaluation. His problem has not been identified to date. The parents are over-anxious about their child. They frequently ask, "Why can't Johnny read? Will he be a first grader all of his life?" John has been in our school for two years. He has gained a year and a half in academic growth. He is a "slow learner" at best. He does not remember what he learned from day to day, which further complicates his problem.

John was a surprise, late baby born to middle aged parents. The mother carries the role of head of the family. The father, neurotic and difficult, does not like to work for a regular salary and prefers to dig an illusive oil well. He also says, "Women can't be trusted." He drives an expensive car, but refuses to have his wife's older car repaired. The water pump leaks. He thinks that if she carries extra water in a gallon can in the car he will be able to control her actions to some extent while he is away.

John idolizes his father and likes nothing better than to go off camping with him to "the oil well" and watch the digging go on, and on, and on—and miss school! The father often promises to take John with him and frequently breaks his word. If John can't go this time—he can dream. He does dream a great deal of the time.

Problem: John was brought to the Special Education Center in order to "learn." Especially in order to "learn to read." Many reading methods were tried unsuccessfully. The Fernald method was the best, as it included writing about a subject of interest to him. John wrote about oil wells, rigging, machinery and camping out on the desert. His vocabulary was high. He gained approximately one academic year during the first winter at school. The second winter he had regressed, but he managed to climb up to third grade level. However, he still tired easily and remembered little. He was listless, bored and without affect. We recommended psychiatric and medical help. Still no improvement was evident. Finally, the ITPA test indicated such a disparity between his chronological age and his visual-motor ability age, that I decided to have a new eye examination.

The family doctor had been an optometrist and not an ophthalmologist. He did not make the proper diagnosis. After two careful examinations by a qualified ophthalmologist, we learned that John could see perfectly—well enough to read *at six feet away* from the printed page. The ophthalmologist did not think that glasses would help John at this time, so we arranged a way to teach him by placing his books on a music stand at the proper distance from his eyes. The sessions were very short at first.

The immediate change in John was startling. The realization that he was not "retarded," "brain damaged" or "neurologically impaired," but, instead, that he could see adequately at a distance relaxed the family pressure. They accepted him, encouraged and loved him temporarily. John started to read the Cowboy Sam series easily, happily and was able to retain what he read without trouble. "Now he will catch up," the mother said hopefully.

John's whole personality and behavior changed overnight. He became a happy child. He teased me and played tricks on his teachers. He told me that he had been frustrated (he used the term) and that his eyes had hurt him every time he tried to read. He said that he had tried hard in order to please his parents and often had become "*so* discouraged." Before, he had not wanted to play with the other children. Now, he couldn't wait for recess. His appetite improved, he gained weight and he was anxious and willing to catch up in his school work, now that he *knew* he could see. His posture improved, his energy increased and his muscle tone strengthened.

At school, his teachers helped him to fulfill his potential. He improved daily. Less daydreaming occurred. His imagination and ingenuity became more realistic and objective. At home, he found outlet for his new energy in digging a fort with his friends: "The Mole" emerged from his hole.

School ended in June. I asked John to come down to see me after a six-week vacation. Pressure at home, broken promises by his father who did not take him camping had returned John to his cave (temenos). "The Mole" took refuge once again. A week later he returned and showed progress. Airplanes were flying over a mound to the left and to the right (see slide #1).

I felt that John could take a challenge of self direction. I gave him a calendar to use when or if he read some of the books he liked. This idea was to be a secret between us. He was on his own. He came to see me two days later and whispered, "I read two times; two pages." The next time I saw him three weeks later, he made a sand picture (slide #2). He had continued to read for himself and had marked the calendar.

Summary: Before the ophthalmologist's examination, John could not resolve his problems. His ego could not constellate. It fluctuated, but the stigma of "retarded" and the family anxiety sapped his libidinal energy and left him helpless. After his visits to the new doctor, the weight of these combined difficulties lifted from John's skinny shoulders and freed him. This enabled him to develop as a person, as well as in his school work. Our relationship (transference) became stronger. I was an ally and could be depended on to help him achieve and stand on his own feet. Pieces of the puzzle began to form a whole (ego), and complexes, which had formerly blocked progress of the process of integration, were removed. Fun took the place of frustration. The ego constellated and strengthened daily. It became visible to the point of becoming defensive and healthily aggressive. Non-verbal secrets were no longer necessary between us, as John could communicate verbally and freely. He felt safe. He began to take responsibility for his own acts and to accept his visual handicap sufficiently to cope with his learning problems. Regardless of his parents' anxiety, he began to move more freely. His psychic energy (libido) began to flow.

If his process continues and firms up, he is on his way. At the end of next year, we can re-estimate progress and ability. The Mole may make it. He is no longer a prisoner burrowing underground. Perhaps he is no longer a mole. Transformation is in process.

*   *   *

In order to objectify the feelings and depressive process which John had been going through, I used the Sandbox Technique to measure and evaluate progress, as seen. The process of healing and "becoming" (integration) experienced by John indicated that his ego had constellated. The slides to which I referred have been obtained over a period of nine months of the school year. Before the problem of visual defect and dysfunction had been identified by the specialist, the child experienced untold frustration, as well as the trauma of being labeled "retarded," a stigma many children suffer from wrong diagnosis. I knew that his functioning ability surpassed the numerical I.Q. of 112 which I had previously obtained. He was able to invent a gadget for my tripod which no photographer had been able to suggest in New York or San Francisco. He later instructed his father how to make it. Several tests pointed to a visual-motor lag in comparison with other areas of testing. Finally, the ITPA test indicated such a disparity between his C. A. and his visual and visual-motor age development that it demanded further ophthalmological investigation. The E.E.G. had shown no specific information concerning brain damage and the Graham-Kendall indicated only a borderline score above "average" at the age of eight, with *slight* organic (visual-motor) problems. These also improved on second try.

The behavior definitely indicated a depressed child with low affect, no motivation and no success or progress in class work. The sandbox slides showed occasional sparks of progress, but the ego constellation fluctuated. It came and went with the mood of the day. A complete reversal of this picture occurred when the boy was examined by the ophthalmologist. With the stigma of "retarded child" removed, the parents showed less anxiety. As pressure decreased, the objective evidence in the sandbox pictures was marked.

LARRY

ADOPTED NEUROLOGICALLY IMPAIRED

Larry is a slight boy with blue eyes and light hair. He is adopted. He is presently seven years old. His large, thin-lipped mouth rarely smiles. Because of inactive muscles, his lips cannot pucker, making his smile rigid. Larry has an elfin quality which is hard to describe and a mischievous look when he knows he has been successful. He is the younger of two boys, both adopted. His wealthy parents give the boys too many gifts. Material objects are no substitute for love. Since Larry is "handicapped" they over-compensate, unaware of the fact that they assume misplaced guilt. To his parents Larry is slow in learning to read. His emotional and physical handicaps are not recognized. The boy has had to cope with this attitude by constantly reaching out for security and love through attention-getting techniques and psuedo-ego development—without consideration of his true feelings. He hides them successfully from his family. His teachers call him "hyperactive." He cannot sit still or concentrate on any task for more than a few minutes at a time. Or, he uses the "It's too hard, I can't do it," game to hide his insecurity and helplessness.

At birth, the physician declared him to be normal and healthy, but as he grew, a developmental lag became evident in walking and talking—possible indications of slight brain dysfunction. There seemed to be minimal neurological impairment and some spasticity in his right side. The defects had not been identified specifically. Since he was an adopted child, the parents felt doubly responsible. They had tried to do everything within their understanding for the boy with the exception of accepting the problem. They attributed his slow learning capacity to "retardation," and were only interested in having him "learn to read." To this end he was pushed mercilessly. In self defense, Larry withheld his true personality. Instead, he substituted a clown-like behavior. Laughing at himself, he would smile a rictus smile, saying "Hi" or "Yes" or "No, I can't do that, it's too hard."

Larry was first brought to the Center for evaluation when he was four years old. I noticed at once that Larry would not follow directions, would not obey, "Now dear, do what Mrs. R. tells you to do. Try!" He was "hyperactive" to extreme.

I sat on the floor in order to keep him with the Stanford-Binet box of testing materials (an intelligence test), and to be able to reach him as he moved around from chair to desk top. He tried to climb the wall, but gave that up after a few attempts. He would not settle down. It was difficult to interest him with the test materials long enough to be able to check his intelligence. I arrived at a score of 58%. I believed him capable of a higher functioning ability than was shown by the numerical score, since he could frequently outmaneuver me. (At that time, we did not have the ITPA, which would have indicated a more accurate picture of his deficit.) I noticed that he had a speech defect. The neurological impairment on his right side carried through to his tongue, lip and facial muscles. This spasticity resulted in blurred speech and a strained smile. His tongue tip and lip muscles were not sufficiently active to produce a good "l," "d," "n" and "t." "W" and "oo" were also impaired sounds as a result of the lip structure. His breath stream was not well coordinated and he could not whistle—a norm which should be achieved by this age. Clear articulation was not possible.

He did not *play*. His gross and fine muscle coordination were poor. Pressure from his parents had submerged his ego. He was nobody. In order to save face, he refused to make any effort towards learning of any kind. So, Larry met with failure after failure and it is not surprising that he became discouraged and refused to try.

Between the time he was tested and 1969, he attended the Montessori school and first grade. He also experienced intensive neurological testing, demanding specific, timed exercises at home. The mother was unable to direct them as her husband was also ill.

Larry tried everything to attract attention, from tantrums and fury to fawning for approbation. He was a pathetic child. The mother still refused to accept the fact that there were many reasons why Larry *refused* to read. It was his only defense. At least, he was being given negative attention. Why should he give up his most useful weapon?

He finally gave up. "I can't," was his continuous reaction. He became so inhibited that he literally refused to try anything new. The result was a negative, helpless, hyperactive and objectionable child. When he became too frustrated, he would threaten to tell his mother, and often she came to us in the morning saying that Larry had told her a story which had no foundation—another attention-getting touch. She did not trust us. Throughout the year we never felt that we could communicate with her. She would say, "Yes," look blank and "Why can't he read?" or, "When will he learn?" Over and over we would explain, "When and if his problems resolve." Larry had no visual or auditory memory. We had to go ahead and try to help him without parental understanding. Though difficult, it was all that could be done in order to help the child overcome his problem.

He was tutored and given special reading help as well as training in other areas. The sandbox was started as a speech tool, not as psychotherapy. The word "psychotherapy" was too threatening to the parents. There was "nothing wrong with him emotionally." We had to be careful of our terminology. The same question came up repeatedly. "Yes, we notice his improvement, but when will he learn to read?" They refused to accept an interview with our consultant psychiatrist.

After two years of working with Larry, motivation and behavior improvement were noticeable in school. Larry was able to persist at a task longer, and occasionally finish a project. His speech improved. He became more intelligible. The tongue tip became active, and he was able to produce "t," "d," "n," and "l" correctly. The lips began to pucker. "Oo" and "w" were possible now. The whistle, not as yet constant or complete, was beginning to come about occasionally as the diaphragm sustained the air column and the lips formed a tiny enough channel.

Larry had not quite been able to synchronize his motions with music, but as his gross muscle coordination improved he was able to beat the drum rhythmically with music.

The sandbox therapy began with complete chaos (see slide #3).

The sand itself had no form. All objects were placed in it without logic, grouping or classification. This continued for several months, but as other problems resolved slowly, Larry began to produce whole concepts. Occasionally, I would say, "Let's just put in one story today." (I have found that with disturbed, brain damaged children, too much freedom of choice cannot be permitted.) Limits are needed at first and welcomed. Slowly, month after month Larry began occasionally to produce his own stories. Chaos diminished and order appeared. The ego was gestating. It finally took shape after eight to nine months (see slide #4). Progress also showed in his painting, in his application in class, in his fine muscle work (printing and crayoning and cutting) and in his behavior. He was a happier child. Socially, he was accepted by his peers. He felt liked and appreciated. Values about family wealth, swimming pools and the like were more his own, less artificial and more realistic.

He was pleased that he could carry out his own ideas. This was apparent in the sandbox or in other creative class work and was verbalized through story dictation to the teacher.

Again, the mother demanded conferences with the educational director who constantly tried to reassure her that some day, perhaps Larry might learn, but not until these basic problems had been met and corrected, resolved and improved. This was happening slowly, but the home pull negated and impeded progress of much that happened in school, especially when the family took off unexpectedly for camping trips with the bright older brother. Larry did insist on practicing his exercises at home in spite of the family. This took ego strength!

The sandbox therapy measured his improvement visibly. One day, Larry spent one hour gluing pebbles on paper outlining the picture of a lamb. His pride in accomplishment was pathetic. He wanted to take the effort home and sleep with it. He had never been able to concentrate more than fifteen minutes or less on any project before. We were quite astonished and pleased. To him it indicated success.

He was removed from the school the following year with no explanation. Hopefully, Larry may be ready to learn to read after all. His visual memory was poor, but may improve in time, as the ITPA tests indicated. If the minimal brain dysfunction could be resolved sufficiently, the rest may follow.

MICHAEL

HIDDEN TREASURE

This is the story of a brave little boy who put up a fight to be recognized and appreciated. Recognition is important to small people. It tells them *who* they are, and who *cares* about them. What they *make* is important, too, as non-verbal communication. Young ones strive to be understood by adults in many ways: tantrums, loving sweetness, possessiveness, stubbornness or crying without reason. Using this indirect language, they are manipulating and playing on adults' emotions. Called attention-getting techniques, these are behavior patterns characteristic of hyperactive or emotionally upset children. It is actually a method of expressing the need to be *recognized* as a person—an entity. In addition, those with brain damage or neurological dysfunction further complicate the picture. The following is the story of Michael or the unrecognized, buried treasure.

Michael was six years and two months old when he came to the Center for the first time. He was small for his age with large, dark eyes. He was *very* quiet. He said nothing, and looked volumes. He took in everything. You could see and feel the "wheels going around." A retarded child does not look alert. A brain damaged child is not looking. He may look, but he does not see. He may listen, but he does not hear. I observe these characteristics in my office when children are brought in to see me with or without parents. The purpose of my initial interview is to gather history and for observation. On the child's part, this first meeting is a time for experiencing and testing me out. Michael looked, observed, took in and measured me well. He said nothing. He *could* talk. His articulation was perfect, perhaps *too* exact. He was not hyperactive, there was no brain dysfunction, no neurological damage evident so far. Later, in the playground, I observed good physical coordination in skipping, running, climbing and walking. There were no gross motor difficulties, which I always take into consideration if a question of minimal brain dysfunction is as yet unidentified by the neurologist or pediatrician. Diagnosis? Still a question. If the physician sends the child in for observation, I start by checking gross motor coordination and continue through fine motor skills. I then test intelligence and academic ability. Michael showed no symptoms of physical difficulty. After a few periods of observation, we went through my list of *Sing It and Do It* or motor exercises, speech test and audiometric measurement. He drew me a picture of a boy (the Goodenough test). It was meticulously done. On the Goodenough scale, the picture revealed the level of about eight years of age.

We made another appointment for further evaluation. He said he would like to come (nodded his head). A time was set for testing: I.Q. (Intelligence Quotient) and S.Q. (Social Quotient), and another version of I.Q. which may be called Imagination Quotient, using the sandbox. I feel this is an equally important consideration to note, as the imagination is *their* kingdom.

Michael's chronological age was six years two months. His ITPA test indicated a four-year-old score for *verbal* expression. His *perceptual* age score was: auditory, eight years four months, and visual, eight years ten months, implying a gifted child, though he might be called a slow learner in some areas. His emotional problem would account for the deficiency in these areas.

Yet he was being labeled as retarded, brain damaged and speech handicapped. His father had become so exasperated by his lack of verbal expression and "inability" to learn to read at first grade level, that he was "beating" Michael emotionally with, "Why *won't* you learn? . . . Are you dumb? Are you retarded?" Verbal beatings hurt deeply, especially from one you love, and whose approbation is your emotional lifeline (father). So, he came to the Center for "remedial reading." I sensed that the problem stemmed from lack of recognition and appreciation of gifts that were not listed in the academic field. If these could be identified, appreciated and given approbation, the child might begin to use other avenues of learning, which would satisfy his father and gain him his rightful place in the family, the oldest son. His two younger brothers (2½, 3½) were very active and more the "average" children. They were, of course, a real threat to Michael in his father's affection, for which he vied and yearned. Poor Michael. If he were denied his place as Number One Son, what then?

We conferred with the parents. The father, a successful Spanish-American, self educated businessman, came in, carefully dressed in fashionable men's style. He was self-conscious and ill at ease. The mother was over-anxious to hear the results of the evaluation. My remarks emphasized the fact that in many areas Michael was developmentally *above* his age level; however, he was a quiet boy and needed much encouragement to show his true colors. Helping him would require family and school cooperation, as well as creative therapy. His quiet behavior indicated strong emotional difficulties, anxieties and hopelessness. This quietness was not a special problem, but an expressive one, a plea for understanding and a dangerous barrier to growth of his personality. Michael needed appreciation, love and encouragement. I did not give his parents numerical scores or a scientific appraisal of my young friend (for we had become *friends* during our sessions). He had found friends among his peers and teachers at the school. He was allowed to make a kite which he drew, invented and could fly. He had been permitted to draw pictures of his own ideas!

Michael had been to a parochial school for a few months, where he had to "sit and LEARN . . . or else." Those were the *rules*. Large group numbers were felt to be a real part of the discipline problem. Teachers were assigned 40-60 first graders. Knowing this, the strict atmosphere is more understandable. Michael was too bright to be inhibited by the rules. He escaped by daydreaming.

Michael was exposed to Sandbox Therapy. He was shown the miniatures on shelves along with the sandboxes. He was asked to choose the sandbox he wished to use, then to pick out the miniatures he wanted to include in his picture. He did, time after time. The slides cannot give you the sense of intensity with which he worked. The directedness and the imagination involved in his creativity indicated anything but a dumb child (see slide #5). The ingenuity he used and the clarity with which he explained his complex projects amazed me (see slide #6). His parents still did not recognize him as a gifted child! The gift of imagination did not seem to have meaning or *value* to them. For this he was given no recognition or appreciation.

Michael *really* learned that year. He enjoyed his school work. He contributed to group projects. He was looked up to by his peers. He enjoyed the sandbox. His efforts were appreciated.

The next year he was again placed in a Parochial School. Hopefully, his experience at the Special Education Center will fortify him permanently.

WARREN

EMOTIONAL AND PHYSICAL DISABILITY

Warren is a handsome little boy of eight. He has brown eyes, light hair, and is well proportioned physically though somewhat slight in build. His right eye turns outwards, he cannot gallop on both sides. His right leg is "lazy," so he overuses his left. He is left-handed. There seems to be some slight neuro-muscular handicap on his whole right side. In spite of this evidence, he has not yet been diagnosed or reported as having slight brain dysfunction. His speech is also impaired. He is having speech therapy and is mugging, and protruding his tongue unnecessarily. The emphasis on tongue action sounds has been overdone. He has become self-conscious of his handicap and tries too hard in order to please his parents. He is over-conscientious and he over compensates in all areas. He is pathetically in need of love and appreciation, demanding this constantly through his behavior. They have termed him "slow," "retarded" and "hyperactive." These terms do not describe Warren. He may be slow at learning to read, since his eyes do not "track" and the right eye cannot fix and track with his left. Even though he wears glasses to read, they do not seem to help. He is also slow in games and cannot compete with his playmates as he moves awkwardly and cannot see well to catch a ball. However, he climbs trees, ladders and tries to jump rope, becomes frustrated at his failures and goes into a tantrum; stamping and crying, hitting out if anyone tries to calm him down.

Warren has other problems—his family. He has a cute, petite, bright-eyed, blond sister two years younger than himself. She gets much attention. Warren has considered this. He decided that being a cute little girl might gain him attention and acceptance (see slide

#7. He identifies strongly with his sister and minces along, tosses his head, and would love to take ballet lessons in which his sister shines. He starts to do *entre chats*, turns and pirouettes if any rhythmic music is on the record player. "Fantasia," of the Nutcracker Suite had to be deleted as it overstimulated him to such a degree that he would jump up in class and start his antics. He could, however, become a good dancer. I tried to turn his gestures into more masculine ones by suggesting fighting to music as pyric dances of the ancient Greeks, or Scotch sword dances, but this was later. It took over a year to improve Warren's coordination and his ability to use his right side as well as to correct his speech habits. He did *Sing It and Do It* rhythms compulsively each day. "Am I doing right? I'm trying very hard!! I can do this well!!" Continuous remarks like these accompanied every exercise, a pathetic cry for recognition and attention. He talked incessantly and disturbed the group, so some of it had to be curbed. In order to overcome his almost phobic insecurity, he was given individual tutoring, and opportunities for Sandbox Therapy. He could concentrate better without peer competition, and in a small room. He was so aware of sound and visual stimuli that it was difficult for him to focus attention in a regular classroom. In fact, that was the main reason for his being referred to the Special Education Center.

The first year with us was spent mainly in reducing his poor speech habits, resolving the motor coordination deficiency on his right side, improving his concentration and lengthening his attention span and building his general health and behavior. Much improvement was noted.

During the second year he continued to improve. He learned cursive writing, to follow directions, to express himself and to control his temper, since frustration was reduced, this came about naturally.

Through viewing a sequence of slides, it was noted at first that perseveration was evident as a symptom of brain damage. As the year progressed, he developed a truly creative approach which indicated emotional progress and definite creative-imaginative ability. Miniature objects began to gain logical arrangement, order and ingenuity (see slide #8). He could not keep still or stop talking in class, but when on his own, he was quiet and could work with concentration for longer periods.

In the meantime, his mother and father were having problems. There was talk of separation and divorce. Warren showed his anxiety by progressive hyperactive behavior; phobic at times and quite irrational. His drawing regressed to the former illogical, sketchy illusory forms of his first attempts of that first year. Then came summer school, and he settled down to better work. He had more freedom and outdoor recreation to take up his nervous energy. The hours were shorter and his peer group less diversified.

Warren's third winter in school was a difficult one for him, and for those of us concerned with his welfare and progress. The divorce of his parents was accomplished. This brought further anxiety and increased insecurity. Warren was almost unmanageable. He talked incessantly and could not settle down to his work. His mother went to work full time, she developed an atttiude of independence, rejecting her home responsibilities. She had never acknowledged that he had emotional problems. She felt that sight was his only problem, which caused him to be slow in reading and other school work. "Nothing else is wrong with him!" She refused to see our consultant psychiatrist. She did accept the guidance of our educational director, since he was more objective and could discuss Warren's academic program instead of the unsavory emotional difficulties.

Warren went to a baby-sitter after school. He did not go home until his mother called for him. He showed more and more disorientation. His drawings were quite unrealistic and confused. They were machines that went off. They represented small figures, part man and part dwarf (fantasy). They were quite illogical and unrealistic. He had learned to read. This pleased his mother and did offer periods of quiet and interest. Then the ophthalmologist decided to operate on the eye muscles for cosmetic reasons, to see if the eye difficulty could be corrected. The child was taken to the hospital and went through the process of muscle tightening on his right eye. He had to wear a patch over his eye for a week. He could not see. He turned his head constantly to try to focus his good eye. He was so nervous that he went to pieces completely and screamed from frustration. One particular phobia was his terror when anyone threatened to pop a plastic or paper bag. He would have hysterics and scream. At times he could not do his rhythms or gain physical relaxation from exercise. The child became prepsychotic; we were worried. Pictures in the sandbox regressed and became illogical. We could not communicate with the mother as she refused to accept the situation. At this time his grandmother called for him after school on some days and added to his anxiety. She threatened him with the wrath of God, Hell and the like. If he were *good* he would go to heaven and God would love him. If not, Hell and the Devil was the answer. Overstimulation, anxiety and insecurity were intensified. Hoping to avoid a serious break, we thought that because of his love for the Nutcracker Suite, moving or dancing to some of the themes would relax him. Instead, I noticed that he became over-stimulated by it. He continued to dance around at home. His mother requested that we delete music and rhythms. The sandbox did give him quiet and an outlet for his imagination and creative energy. At times he still would go into paroxysms of rage and was quite uncontrollable. After going to San Francisco, to the psychiatric conference, I had studied new ways for helping the autistic child, which I decided to use for Warren.

In the middle of one of his uncontrollable tantrums, I held him and spoke to him quietly for fifteen minutes. Finally, he relaxed completely and said, "I'm through." He was happier and went into the classroom to work and read. It was his first relaxed period for many months. He knew that someone cared enough to hold him and give him a sense of security which he was seeking. The next time I tried holding him, the tantrum was shorter and less violent. When he was ready, he went off on his business and remained relaxed for several days.

His mother is still unable to accept the child's emotional reaction to his problems or his evident progress in spite of them. She speaks of finding a residential school for him, but it would be sad to allow such a child to be forgotten and to permit him to fulfill his potential without love and acceptance at home.

The mother remarried and the family constellation has greatly improved. Warren feels cared for and loved by the stepfather. There seems to be hope.

WILLIAM

REACTION FROM EMOTIONAL TRAUMA

A GIFTED CHILD

William will be eight in January. He is a tousle-headed boy with light hair (longish in front, so he can see out when he *wants* to and in back so he doesn't *have* to wash behind his ears). He is slight and well-proportioned. His muscle tone is poor, unless he wants to hit you. He has keen blue eyes that glance quickly all around him. He takes in a great deal and doesn't miss essentials—or—he is off day dreaming in his own world.

He is imaginative, aware of all that is beautiful, and intensely creative when working on a task that interests him. He manipulates his environment and those that are a part of it. His teachers, usually, fall for his wiles and blandishments and are not always aware of his tricks.

His mother died of self-inflicted arsenic poisoning when he was five. "Your mother died of rat poison!", the children in his class tease. At home, he is over-cared for by a motherly father whom he hates or—to the other extreme, neglected by incompetent and frequently changing baby-sitters. He has a very bright subteen aged sister who gets A's in the parochial school which she attends. To demonstrate his feelings about the loss of his mother, his dislike of his father, and possibly sibling resentment of his sister, he refuses to learn in school and defecates daily in his clothes. "Enchoprisis" is the technical name. He has been going to a psychiatrist for the purpose of curing the problem. Play therapy under a counselor (Mother Substitute) has been of no avail to date.

William has since entered our Center where the efforts of psychiatrist, psychologist, counselor and his teachers combined in order to work out a plan for his improvement. He is presently on a "clean it up yourself" routine which he accepts silently but—he does not change, much. At times, there are days when cleaning up is unnecessary, but they are rare, and hopefully, they will be on the increase. Added to this pecularity, he *will not* learn, although he is quite capable of doing so, as all tests indicate above average intelligence. An E.E.G. showed no brain damage. Sight, hearing and perception are adequate. Memory is poor, both visual and auditory. He sees and hears, but only what he wishes to. I have known this to happen to children (or adults) who have had an emotional shock. They create a block to painful memories. William realizes well what this means to his father and overbearing paternal grandmother. She is only interested in the fact that a child *must* be up in his school grades if he is not to be labeled "retarded," that dreaded term, which means so little. So William's unusual creative gifts go unappreciated at home. At school, since we take imagination and creative ability into consideration as indication of superiority, we recognize William's potential. His maternal grandmother is more understanding and less rigid. She is superior intellectually, however, and rejects William's father since she blames him for her daughter's death. The two grandmothers do not speak to each other. They are both over-anxious for William to *learn*. "We know you can, dear." At school we also know he can and will *when* he decides to.

When William came to school in September, he accepted it. He had previously attended a private school as well as the Free School directed by a "school rebel" who went to England to study the Summerhill school system. For William, there was perhaps too much freedom allowed for which he was not ready. He had been brought up as a Roman Catholic in a structured program. Too much freedom would confuse rather than help William. I have observed that children with disabilities need *more* rather than less direction to begin discipline. William needed the security of limits.

When William came to school, his muscle tone was poor. He could neither push nor pull with energy. His whole attitude was flaccid. It took several months of rhythmic exercises (*Sing It and Do It*) to bring these up to healthy tone. I gathered that his diet at home was largely composed of what he wanted to eat, when he wanted to eat it. There was little supervision during the daytime other than the baby-sitter. He was free to take a city bus home each day in order to foster a sense of personal responsibility, as well as to develop a feeling for time and schedule. If he missed the bus, he liked to walk home, a distance of several miles. He knew quite a bit about the city, and would tell me about it when I called for him each morning to take him to school. I decided to use time with him this way as a daily twenty-minute period of indirect therapy which would be of value to us both as he progressed towards goals (reading). He either wanted to talk or kept silent. He liked to remark about buildings and whether he liked them or not. We discussed why and what made them good or why he did not like them. His observations were excellent. He had a feeling for design, structure and proportions. I took different ways to school in order to give him variation of scenes. He could decide which way to take on some days. Other days, I would say we had to go to the post office and would give him the opportunity to mail my letters and distinguish between the Air Mail and Local mail boxes. He usually got it right. He learned to read signs and to know A. from L. He was aware of my tricks. At times, he "forgot" or "could not see," in order to get my goat. But we both laughed, and he knew that I knew what he was up to. From these daily trips I learned a lot about William. He was bright, unusually so, and could outsmart most adults. His inner world was definitely more interesting to him than what he saw in the "real" world. It was safer, too. I felt that his fantasy, if used creatively, could be a *tool*, not a handicap. But, he must learn to distinguish between them appropriately.

Socially, William treated the other children as friends or foes, varying from day to day. He hated and he liked. He accepted group activities one day or refused to cooperate on another day. His behavior was as ambivalent as his moods. He would manipulate teachers skillfully in order to get what he wanted.

The school program followed the usual curriculum, but periods of work were shortened and the discipline made more flexible in order to meet the individual needs of each child. Individual help was stressed. This, William would play for and get! He would play helpless, "I can't do it. I don't remember," and the like. It worked well with most teachers. With me, however, he realized that I knew exactly what he was up to (but he could fool me, too, at times).

No child is "retarded" if he is that cunning. William was inclined to daydream and be disruptive when bored. I have noticed this with gifted children, who get answers long before others. William enjoyed drawing or painting pictures. He was outstanding in any art project, in inventing, imagining and using ingenuity to produce original concepts. He would illustrate a story or build a block castle of unusual complexity.

I started William in the sandbox in his second month. At first, his sand pictures were unformed. The sand was loose and without structure. As time went on, his forms evolved and became firm (see slide #9). Academic improvement was noticed. Some gain in numbers and reasoning began to show. Occasionally, a gain in reading or spelling occurred. It varied and was definitely influenced by the home events. One day, the cat had kittens at home. He was awed and interested by the process of birth which he had watched and was able to describe to me vividly on the way to school. Another time he had been promised a puppy from the animal Shelter for his birthday. He picked one out—tall and with a long tail. The babysitter refused to have a dog in the house. He was denied the pup. Grownups were difficult to understand. His father had broken his promise. That day the lessons were all off and he drifted off into his safe world of fantasy. The Mouse picture in the sandbox was a result. "It's my world and no one can come in it unless I want them to." The mouse Queen theme was repeated in paintings, and he wrote a story about it. It seemed to have a hold on him for nearly a week. Finally, in order to break the spell, I decided to take steps to help him into reality and to leave the world of fantasy. On our way to school, I tried a practical approach. We discussed buildings, apartments, hotels and looked at another building which was being torn down bit by bit, causing much comment among the "Old Guard" who wanted to preserve it for a museum and posterity, etc. Gradually, he began to observe the concrete aspects of buildings, and invented and produced some in the sandbox. He embellished them with balconies, gardens and pools (see slide #10). One day, he announced, "I'm either going to be an architect or a cartoonist." There was slight progress in reading and school work. His muscle tone improved so that he could push anyone down, especially if they talked about rat poisoning and his mother. If a boy started a fight, he would fight back and protect himself. Before, he cried and ran from the attack. One day, he started to read primers for pleasure. He said he had read two to his grandmother and she was happy about it. Perhaps pressure will relax and he can begin to learn at his own pace. I feel that the level of learning is high already, but he has much to overcome in his life conditions at home. His father's attitude must also change. Nothing seems to touch him, however. He seems to understand William's problem, yet does not follow through. The boy must make it alone. This will not be easy, but I believe he can do it with proper guidance. His spring tests showed a 3.2 grade level. We are hoping that before the end of the next school term William can be entered in a regular school at his chronological age level.

Two years later: His father has remarried a wife of the Roman Catholic faith and they have bought a home in the country. William was sent to a parochial school where he is reported to be doing well in all school subjects.

A child with hearing impairment cannot speak because he has not heard the sounds or words that make up speech. The auditory input necessary for the development of speech has been cut off. The usual method for human communication is verbal. Language is the avenue of understanding another individual. It must be encouraged in order for communication to develop satisfactorily. It is psychologically important as it will influence mental and social maturation. We grow through interacting with others, imitation and experience. Usually, verbalization—speech—is the tool by which we communicate our needs, ideas, emotions and form our concepts. A hearing loss of any degree is a serious handicap. A total hearing loss (profound) may cause developmental retardation and only through great patience and discipline can it be remedied.

There are two main remedial philosophies for the deaf child:

1) The manual language may be taught as a substitute for speech. Using fingers and sight compensate for lack of hearing. It limits the individual to communicate with only other handicapped individuals or their teachers—a limited group, similarly deprived.

2) The Aural-oral method uses any residual hearing the child may possess. (Only 20% of those who experience hearing loss are totally deaf.) The goal of this method is reproduction of words and teaching the child to use sounds in a meaningful

pattern for communication. It is a difficult and slow task to develop sufficient meaningful sounds (words) and vocabulary with which to communicate one's needs, thoughts and ideas— but once achieved, the deaf child is able to lead a more normal life including the ability to maintain a job. He will not be limited to a small group of handicapped individuals or to menial, uninteresting occupations.

Psychologically, the hearing impaired child suffers from experiential deprivation. A lack of stimuli (sound) is evident and response is equally low. He is limited from the start and cannot help but suffer from this limitation. His life is more circumspect. He cannot be as free as the average child. His parents are more anxious about his whereabouts, his actions and what he is doing in order to prevent accidents. He must be constantly watched. He must learn by rote and endless repetition. His freedom is curtailed. Play is limited, if not totally absent. Imagination develops through play and experimentation—exploration. It is vital to learning. The deaf child has few avenues for this activity. He is afraid to explore as a result of lack of opportunity and freedom to experiment.

At the Hearing and Speech Center, an aural-oral school for the hearing impaired child, the director gave us permission to try the sandbox miniature technique of play in the pre-school. These children must develop speech before the age of seven. After that, the optimal learning age is passed and cannot be compensated for.

The purposes for using the Sand Tray were:
1. To encourage verbalization through free play.
2. To encourage concept formation.
3. To develop ideas through use of objects.
4. To express fears or other emotional blocks and reactions.
5. To release tensions and communicate non-verbally.
6. Above all, to have the opportunity for activities and free play in a constructive and meaningful framework.

Photographic slides were taken of each presentation and the sequence over a period of time in order to show the therapist how well the child is progressing. Examples of progress and valuable purpose of the Sand Tray Technique follow.

Maria is an alert, bright-eyed girl of six. She is bilingual. As a result of profound hearing loss, she wears hearing aids to amplify any residual hearing she may have. She has been at the aural pre-school for two years and has learned to speak. Language and vocabulary are good considering her deficiency. It is apparent that her concepts and understanding of action verbs are well developed and meaningful. Maria has an older sister who gives her much help at home, as do her parents.

This fall, those in contact with Maria at the pre-school noticed that she was more withdrawn in the classroom situation than in the previous year. Her mother expressed concern over Maria's fear of sleeping alone and her fear of being alone in the bathroom with the door closed. She reported that Maria had severe nightmares from which she often awoke, screaming. The family was disturbed and mystified by these occurrences. An over-active imagination became evident. Clouds which might be simply picturesque hung in ominous images over Maria's world—forcing her to cover her eyes and run for protection, indoors.

We decided to try the sandbox technique as therapy with Maria. An opportunity for non-verbal expression might relieve some of her imaginary fears. As therapy began, Maria showed a wealth of feelings. She began a meaningful creation in the sandbox, familiarizing herself with some of the animals and surprising us with her vocabulary. When she chose the furry seal I asked where it lived and she mimed swimming. Pushing aside the sand in order to reveal the blue base of the box or "water" she said, "Pool." For symbolic representation of fears or threatening figures she chose a dinosaur and a hippopotamus. The dinosaur fought the hippo and ate several other animals. Then the two demons were partially contained by a fence and were not allowed to escape. After a few sessions a tree sprang up near the fence. As it had been defoliated by the dinosaur in an earlier picture, this was a welcome sign of new life.

For several more sessions, Maria allowed the dinosaurs to direct the progress of her play. Gradually, she spent less time with them, but kept them surrounded by a fence throughout the time she spent involved with other figures (see slide #11). Periodically, friendly miniatures would try to overcome the scary beasts. A white horse emerged from Maria's dream world. Often the white horse stood close to the living tree. During one of her later sessions, Maria acted out a scene, possibly an indication of her own feelings. She mimed that the colt, which lay on the shelf containing numerous miniatures, was crying for its mother, the white horse. The girl figure opened the gate and the horse flew over to the shelf to be re-united with the colt. Together they returned to the fenced enclosure. Maria then turned the sign near the gate to "open" so that it could be read from outside the fence. This was explained with some speech accompanied by mime. Here, an important resolution of Maria's problems began its course.

In the next session, Maria drove off the dinos. They retreated to one end of the box while the human figures directed all the animals into the fenced enclosure.

One day, three student nurses came to observe the sandbox technique while Maria was working in the sand. She continued without interruption showing her self-assuredness and growing ability to concentrate on her own ideas in the presence of strangers.

Gradually Maria's control of threatening ideas improved. In the sandbox, friendly animals and human figures were substituted for the dinos. Maria's final picture preceding the holiday recess showed her progress dramatically. She experimented with new miniatures. She confidently arranged the family: momma and papa together, sister in bed and Maria in *her own* bed. The dinosaurs were tossed out of the picture leaving the white horse to stand guard. At the same time, Maria's teacher mentioned her progress in social classroom interaction. Maria's confidence was developing. Maria's mother informed us that she no longer screamed at night. The nightmares ceased! Maria had dispelled her fear of clouds and would gladly attend trips on cloudy days without clinging to her teacher's hand. She would walk alone.

During the vacation from school and therapy, she had a recurrence of past fears, but after resuming the work in the sandbox, they disappeared. Maria was able to work them out for herself. The sand magic helped her to constellate her ego. In the course of three months, using this medium of creative expression, she could understand her fears, give them shape through meaningful play and finally discard them.

PEDRO

Pedro, a boy of six, is the second of three children. He lives with his mother, older sister and younger brother in a small oil/ranching community. Pedro was referred to the Hearing and Speech Center following a complete medical examination as he was unable to continue in a first grade situation, which he entered after Head Start. His mother had noticed unusual behavior in the preceding four-year period, but until this time had not sought outside help. When Pedro was two and one-half years old, his father left their home. Until this time he had achieved the usual developmental milestones. Following this family break, Pedro ceased verbal communication with his mother and seemed to regress, socially. Other unusual behavior included hand flapping and autistic-like tendencies. Evidently, his father's absence was deeply disturbing to Pedro. He experienced a recent operation for chronic middle ear infection, but suffered no resultant hearing loss. The doctor termed Pedro's behavior, "elective mutism." Until he could express some of his anger over losing his father, Pedro would probably reserve his voice.

Pedro made friends with his speech pathologist, Karen, at the Center. When he began some verbalization, it was Karen's suggestion that they try sandbox sessions. Pedro showed signs of being experientially deprived. So, in addition to his regular speech therapy, Pedro began to play in the sand. We hoped that this type of experience would stimulate speech and concept formation, as well as add to his meagre experiential history.

At first, he was shy, insecure and withdrawn. Karen remained with us during the initial sessions. Gradually, as Pedro became more involved in his productions, he moved from one to three-word phrases. By the fourth or fifth session, he had formed more fluent speech in complete sentences. One especially exciting session occurred when Pedro discovered that he could add water to the already damp sand. (Only once before he had chosen the damp sand—He was carefully staying close to his experience on sure ground—desert country.) Initially, he made a mound and buried a boy figure to the neck saying, "You got the boy. He can't get out . . . They're trying to get the boy out." An idea sprang from the discovery of a new toy —a boat. He was involved, energy flowed. Pedro created a channel the full length of the box and filled it with water. The boat floated until the water seeped through the banks. He gradually incorporated the figures which had begun the picture. The finished creation brought forth great pleasure and a sense of accomplishment (see slide #12). Pedro narrated an exciting story and in the process he liberated the boy figure, himself.

Throughout this progression, we received favorable reports of his verbal communication with his mother and his aunt. He stayed with relatives for the days of his weekly sessions since he commuted by bus approximately 400 miles to the city. Pedro's aunt told us of his improvement in relating to his cousin, during these visits. He also seemed to be gaining more confidence with older people even in foreign situations. Pedro is presently in first grade and he is apparently doing well. He continues speech work and sandbox therapy with us at the Center.

ANDY

The child who "blocks" or whose speech is arhythmic or disfluent is usually called or miscalled—a stutterer. A spasm or block (tonic or clonic) has occurred in his speech mechanism and interrupted fluency. Stuttering may be caused by a neurological defect or dysfunction, emotional trauma, environmental factors or combinations of the above. Another possible cause is poor habit formation when speech is developing in the young child. Much has been written on the subject. No two cases are alike.

Parakinetic behavior (unnecessary body activity) is often observed as part of the stuttering syndrome. Training, or willful control such as stamping the foot, making a fist or a like action are used by individuals to break the tonic block. If the client can be trained not to use these actions as a crutch before it has become set in the neurological pattern, the secondary stage may be avoided.

Children learning to speak may repeat words or syllables in order to perfect their articulation. If this stage of speech development is interfered with, the child becomes anxious, hesitates and loses his natural fluency. If this habit continues too long, parents become anxious and name the hesitancy or repetition "stuttering." A Speech Center is found and according to the advise of the therapist's penchant, therapy is instituted.

Andy, a child of five and one-half years, was brought to the Albuquerque Hearing and Speech Center for evaluation and therapy. The therapist was interested in trying the indirect approach as a beginning. His aunt agreed that the sandbox would be beneficial as he had many emotional problems to work out at home and this might reflect his inner attitude.

After five or six sessions of constructive play, Andy is progressing well with his sandbox experiences. He brings objects from his collection of toys to use in his play and chatters constantly as he works. There seems to be no flaw in his fluency while enjoying the sand play period. He answers questions in complete, flowing sentences. The only noticeable slur is with the word "What" when used as a question. His realistic manipulation of dinosaurs prompts description. While he is in command and telling *his* story, he speaks strongly and without hesitation. The monkey and other creatures have fun, together (see slide #13).

We don't interpret his choice of objects and manipulation of them as seriously as with more pronounced problems. If Andy is able to express his ideas verbally with confidence in this protected situation, he will gradually gain confidence. His speech problem may improve and blocking become less severe. This is already apparent, after several conferences with both his mother and his conscientious and honestly concerned aunt.

BIBLIOGRAPHY

1. Axline, Virginia, *Play Therapy*, Ballantine Books, New York, 1969.
2. Bender, Lauretta, *Child Psychiatric Techniques*, Charles C. Thomas, Springfield, Illinois, 1952.
3. Bowyer, Laura R., *The Lowenfeld World Technique*, Pergamon Press, New York, 1970.
4. Kalff, Dora, *Sandplay*, The Browser Press, San Francisco, 1971.
5. Moustakas, Clark, *Psychotherapy with Children*, Harper, New York, 1959.
6. Neumann, Erich, *The Child*, G. P. Putnam's Sons, New York, 1973.
7. Piaget, Jean, *Play, Dreams and Imitation in Childhood*, W. W. Norton & Co., Inc., New York, 1962.
8. Reed, Jeannette P., "Sing It and Do It," The University of New Mexico Press, Albuquerque, 1948.
9. Stone, Harold, "The Child: His Mind and His Imagination," Offprint from "Spectrum Psychologiae," Racher Verlag, Zurich and Stuttgart, 1965.
10. Sullwold, Edith, "Eagle Eye," *The Well-Tempered Tree: Essays into the Spirit of our Time*, (Jung Foundation), Putnam, 1971.
11. Van Riper, C., *Speech Correction*, Prentice-Hall, Inc., New York, 1947.

THIS BOOK IS SET IN LINOTYPE PALATINO
10 POINT BOOKFACE WITH 12 POINT LEADING
AND IS LITHOGRAPHED ON WARREN'S PATINA
MATTE AND PALOMA MATTE COVER AND PERFECT BOUND BY
DURHAM AND DOWNEY, INC.
BOOK DESIGN AND PRODUCTION SUPERVISION BY
CHAS. S. POLITZ & ASSOCIATES, PORTLAND, OREGON